Y'all
Eat
Yet?

Rose M. Ousley

This book is dedicated to everyone that loves to cook.

To everyone that has to get a meal on the table no matter what.

To my daughter-in-law LaKeesha:
Thank you for being a wonderful mom to my grandsons and an awesome wife to my son.

To Amanda Richardson and Nequoya Streeter:
Thanks so much for your computer expertise.

To my son Shawn:
You are my forever blessing. I love you!

Some Quick Tips

Check each recipe to see if the oven needs to be preheated.

Most casserole dishes can be frozen and cooked later.

Make two casseroles and freeze one for later.

Always read recipes before starting to prep them.

Use leftover meats, potatoes and vegetables in casserole when possible.

Always enjoy every meal!

Recipe & Page

On this page write down your favorite recipes in this book and what page they are located.

Crispy Sesame Chicken

1 Cup of grated parmesan cheese
3lbs of deboned chicken thighs
½ cup melted butter
2 tablespoons sesame seeds
½ cup of bread crumbs

Preheat oven to 350°F

Combine cheese, bread crumbs and sesame seeds. Dip chicken into butter, dredge in bread crumb mixture. Place chicken in a baking dish. Bake at 350°F for 60 minutes or until internal temperature of chicken is 165°F.

Rotel Chicken Bake

3 lbs cooked chicken (cut into bite size pieces)
1 pack of tortillas
1 large onion diced
1 lb grated sharp cheese
1 can of Rotel
1 can mushroom soup
1 cup of chicken broth

In a casserole dish layer chicken, onion, cheese, and tortillas. Repeat until you have 3 layers. In a bowl combine broth, Rotel, and mushroom soup. Pour over ingredients in casserole dish. Bake at 350°F for 25 minutes. Add more cheese on top if you wish.

Creamy Chicken Breast

4 boneless chicken breast cut in half
4 slices of swiss cheese
1 – 10oz can of cream of chicken soup
¼ cup white cooking wine
1 cup of herb seasoning stuffing mix
(crumbled)
¼ cup of butter melted

Preheat oven at 350°F.

Arrange chicken in a casserole dish, top
chicken with cheese. Mix soup and wine.
Spoon over chicken, sprinkle crumbled
stuffing mix over chicken. Drizzle butter on
top. Bake for 45 or until the internal
temperature of the chicken is 165 °F.

Turkey Pasta Casserole

12 oz of ziti pasta
2 cups of cooked bite-sized turkey
      (can be leftover turkey)
½ cup chopped onions
1can of cream of mushroom soup
½ cup of chicken broth
1/8 teaspoon of salt
1/8 teaspoon black pepper
1½ cup of grated sharp cheese

Preheat oven to 350°F

Cook pasta and drain. In a bowl mix
together onions, turkey, soup, broth, salt and
pepper. Add pasta. And mix again. Pour
entire mixture into a greased casserole dish.
Top with cheese.
Bake at 350°F for 30 minutes.

Vegetable Pasta Sweet and Spicy

12 oz of spaghetti noodles
¼ cup apple juice
1 cup chopped onions
2 tablespoons minced garlic
1 large bell pepper (chopped)
1 cup grated carrots
½ cup of broccoli florets
1 tablespoon fresh chives (chopped)
½ cup plain yogurt
3 tablespoons grated parmesan cheese
1/3 cup nonfat ricotta cheese
½ cup sour cream
1/3 cup ground mustard
1 tablespoon honey
A pinch of Salt and pepper to taste
2 tablespoons olive oil

Cook past and drain. In a large skillet over medium heat, add olive oil. When hot, add onions, garlic and apple juice. Cook about 5 minutes. Then add bell peppers, carrots, broccoli, and chive. Cook for 5 minutes. Combine yogurt, cheese, sour cream, mustard, honey, salt and pepper. Serve by mixing with pasta or on a plate with sauce topping pasta. Serve immediately.

Eggplant Casserole

2 medium eggplants cut in one inch pieces
1lb ground beef
1large onion
1 -14oz can of diced tomatoes
A pinch of salt and pepper to taste
½ cup of grated cheese

Fry eggplant slices and set aside. Cook beef and onions together and drain grease. Add tomatoes, salt and pepper to ground beef. Arrange eggplant in casserole dish, add ground beef mixture and spread evenly. Top with cheese. Bake 30 minutes at 375°F.

Tuna Noodle Casserole

2 cups of noodles (cooked)
1 teaspoon salt
7 oz. tuna drained
1 can cream of mushroom soup (10 ounces)
½ cup of milk
8oz. frozen peas
¼ cup bread crumbs
Cooking spray

Preheat oven to 350°F

Spray a 2 quart casserole dish with cooking spray. Cook noodles in salt water and drain. Mix milk and soup. In casserole dish, layer noodles, tuna, peas and soup. Repeat until you have 2-3 layers. Top with bread crumbs. Bake for 35 minutes at 350°F uncovered.

Lobster and Crab Quiche

9 inch pie pan
2 tablespoons finely chopped green onions
1 cup of crab meat
1 cup of cooked lobster meat
1 tablespoon of fresh dill
4 large eggs slightly beaten
1 ¼ cup of half and half
¼ tablespoon pepper
1/8 table spoon salt

Bake pie crust until lightly brown. In a small sauce pan bring half/half to a boil. Sauté onions in butter and spread in the bottom of cooked pie crust. Top with crab and lobster meat, sprinkle with dill. Combine eggs, salt, pepper and half/half. Mix well, pour into pie shell. Bake at 350°F for 25 to 30 minutes or until set.

Oven Hash

3 Medium potatoes peeled and sliced thin
1 lb ground beef
1 small onion chopped
1 can cream of mushroom soup
1 cup of water
1 pack of Fritos
½ lb of grated Colby cheese
Cooking spray

In a skillet combine ground beef and onions. Cook until beef is brown. Spray casserole dish with cooking spray. Place potatoes in bottom of casserole dish. Add cooked hamburger and onion, add soup and water. Crumble Fritos on top and add cheese. Bake at 350°F for 45 minutes.

Stew Beef Pie

2 lbs beef tips, cooked & cut into bite size
pieces
1 cup of chopped celery
1 cup chopped onion
1 cup chopped carrots
1 chopped bell pepper
1 cup of potatoes sliced thin
1 can of beef broth
1 pie crust

Preheat oven to 350°F

In casserole dish, layer beef, add vegetables.
Cover with broth. Top with pie crust. Bake
at 350°F for 45 minutes to 1 hour.

Beef Casserole with Potato Chops

1 lb beef cooked and crumbled
10 oz English peas
2 cups finely chopped celery
10 oz. can mushroom soup
½ teaspoon salt
½ teaspoon pepper
1 small onion chopped
1 cup crushed potato chips

Place beef in casserole dish.
Pour peas over meat.
Sprinkle celery over peas.
In a bowl mix soup, salt, pepper and onions.
Pour mixture evenly into casserole dish.
Top with crushed chips.

Bake at 375°F for 30 to 35 minutes or until
hot and bubbly.

Ricotta Cheese Pie!

1 ½ cup short bread cookie crumbs
1 tablespoon orange zest
2 tablespoons butter melted
3 large eggs
¾ cup of sugar
2 ½ cups of ricotta cheese
1 tablespoon of vanilla extract
½ cup of slivered toasted almonds

Preheat oven to 375°F

In a bowl combine cookie crumbs, orange zest and melted butter. In the bottom and sides of a 9 inch pie pan press the crumb mixture. Bake for 4 minutes on 375°F.
In a second bowl thoroughly mix eggs and sugar together. Blend into the second bowl ricotta cheese, vanilla and almonds until smooth. Pour into crust and bake at 325°F for 40 minutes
 Serve warm.

Sweet and Sour Turkey

4 cups of cooked turkey (cut into cubes)
½ cup of firmly packed brown sugar
1 cup of turkey broth
1/3 cup of vinegar
¼ cup soy sauce
2-tablespoons cornstarch
¾ diced carrots
2 tablespoons vegetable oil
¾ diced bell peppers
¾ cup pineapple chunks
¼ cup of ketchup
1lb of cooked rice

Combine broth, brown sugar, vinegar, soy
sauce, ketchup and cornstarch. Cook over
medium heat, stir until thickened. Remove
from heat. In a skillet with vegetable oil,
sauté carrots for 1 minute, add peppers,
pineapple and turkey. Cook over medium
heat about 5 minutes. Add sauce and simmer
for an additional 5 minutes.
Serve over rice.

Makes 6-8 servings

Holiday Turkey Sandwiches

2 tablespoons of cream cheese
2 table spoons of olive oil mayonnaise
8 slices of whole wheat bread
¼ cup cranberry orange relish
8 thinly sliced roasted turkey breast
4 leaves of green lettuce

Combine cream cheese and mayonnaise in a small bowl, stir until smooth. Spread on four slices of bread. Spread relish on the other four slices of bread. Start with turkey, then lettuce on first slice of bread with cream cheese mixture, top with bread with relish. Slice in half. Serve with grapes, sliced pears and peaches.

Pita Pizza

1- 6 inch pita bread round
2 tablespoons pizza sauce
2 tablespoons shredded mozzarella cheese
5 slices pepperoni

Spread sauce on pita, top with cheese and pepperoni. Bake at 450°F for about 8 minutes or until cheese melts.

Serve with fresh green salad

Turkey Stacks

4 Italian Rolls (split in half)
¼ cup Italian dressing
4 slices cooked turkey
4 slices thinly sliced salami
4 thinly sliced mozzarella cheese
1 cup of roasted red peppers slice.
White pepper

Brush cut side of rolls with dressing. Fold turkey and salami in half, layer on outside of roll with dressing, top with cheese and red peppers, sprinkle with white pepper.

Serve warm or cold.

Goes great with soup!

Ham and Cheese Sliders

8 Hawaiian Rolls split in half
8 slices of honey ham
8 slices American cheese
8 slices Swiss cheese
Ranch dressing
Melted butter

Preheat oven to 325°F

Split rolls in half, brush each cut with ranch dressing, top one side with cheese and ham. Top with remaining rolls. Brush with butter. Place in 325°F oven for 8-10 minutes. Pull apart or slice

Serve with chips or chili

Hawaiian Jalapeño Sliders

12 Hawaiian Jalapeno Rolls
8 ounces of cream cheese (softened)
2 cups of Monterrey jack cheese
6 strips of cooked bacon
½ cup of Rotel
6 thinly sliced slices of roasted chicken breast
Melted butter
Garlic powder

Split rolls in half. Place the bottom part of the roll in a casserole dish. Top with cream cheese, bacon, chicken, Rotel and one cup of Monterrey jack cheese. Top with remaining rolls, brush with melted butter. Sprinkle with garlic powder, top with remaining Monterrey jack cheese. Place casserole dish in oven. Bake for 6-8 minutes. Pull apart or cut.

Serve with Soup!

Chili and Rice dinner

½ lb ground beef
1/3 cup of chopped onions
1 tablespoon chili powder
½ tablespoon dry mustard
10 ounces while kernel corn
1 cup diced chili powder
15 ounces of tomato sauce
½ cup of water
1 cup of minute rice
½ cup shredded cheddar cheese

In a small boiler cook rice. Brown beef and onions in a skillet. Once the meat is brown add spices, corn, pepper, tomato sauce and water. Cover and bring to a boil, stirring occasionally. Stir in rice, reduce heat. Cover and simmer for about 8 minutes, sprinkle with cheese.

Enjoy!

Tater Tot Casserole

1 ½ lbs of ground beef (cooked)
1 medium green onion (chopped)
1 can of cream of chicken soup
1 small pack of frozen tater tots
1 can or cream of celery soup
½ cup of sharp cheese

Line casserole dish with cooked meat.
Sprinkle with onions, add chicken soup and
a layer of tater tots, add celery soup, top
with cheese and remaining tater tots.

Bake at 350°F for 35 minutes

Egg Nog Pound Cake

1 pack of yellow cake mix
1 pack of instant vanilla pudding and pie
filling mix
¾ cup of egg nog
¾ cup of vegetable oil
4 large eggs
½ teaspoon ground nutmeg
Powdered sugar

Preheat oven to 350°F

In large bowl, combine cake mix, pudding
mix, egg nog and oil. Mix at a low speed
until smooth. Add eggs, and nutmeg. Mix on
medium-high speed about 5 minutes. Pour
into a greased and floured Bundt pan. Bake
at 350°F for 45 minutes.
Cool-10 minutes- Remove from pan
Cool completely. Sprinkle with powdered
sugar.

Serve with egg nog or coffee.

Pumpkin Pie Crunch

1 can pumpkin (16 ounces)
1 can evaporated milk
3 large eggs
1 ½ cups of sugar
4 teaspoons of pumpkin pie spice
½ teaspoon salt
1 yellow cake mix
1 chopped nuts
1 butter melted
Whipped topping

Preheat oven to 350°F

Grease bottom of 13x9 baking pan. In a large bowl mix together pumpkin, milk, eggs, sugar, spices and salt. Pour in a greased pan, sprinkle dry cake mix evenly over pumpkin mixture. Top with pecan. Drizzle with melted butter. Bake at 350°F for 50 to 55 minutes or until golden. Cool completely. Serve with whipped topping.

Makes 16-20 servings.

Snicker doodles

1 package of yellow cake mix
2 large eggs
¼ cup of oil
1 teaspoon of ground cinnamon
3tablespoons of sugar

Preheat oven to 375°F

Grease baking sheet. Combine sugar and cinnamon in a medium bowl. Combine cake mix, eggs and oil in large bowl. Mix until smooth. Shape in one inch balls and place 2 inches apart on baking sheet. Flatten with bottom of a glass or coffee cup. Bake at 375°F for 8 to 9 minutes or until set. Let cool. Make about 3 dozen (for all cookie)

Cool cookies one minute on baking sheet, move to cooling rack to cool completely before serving.

Spicy Oatmeal Raisin Cookies

1 Package of Spice Cake Mix
4 Egg whites
1 cup of uncooked quick cooking oat (not instant oat)
½ cup of vegetable oil
½ cup of raisins

Preheat oven to 350°F

Grease baking sheet. Combine cake mix, egg whites, oats and oil in a large bowl. Mix well. Stir in raisins. Drop by teaspoonful onto prepared baking sheet.

Bake at 350°F for 7 to 9 minutes or until lightly browned.

Cool before serving.

Golden Oatmeal Muffins

1 package of butter recipe golden cake mix.
1 cup uncooked quick cooking oats (not instant oats)
¼ teaspoon salt
¾ cup of milk
2 large eggs
2 tablespoons butter

Preheat oven to 400°F

Use paper liners in 24 count muffin tin. Combine cake mix, oats and salt in a large bowl. Add milk, eggs and butter, stir until moistened. Fill muffin cups 2/3 full. Bake at 400°F for 13 minutes or until golden brown. Cool in pan 10 minutes.

Serve with honey or jam

US Dry Volume Measurements

MEASURE	EQUIVALENT
6 teaspoon	dash
teaspoon	a pinch
aspoons	1 Tablespoon
cup	2 tablespoons (= 1 standard coffee scoop)
cup	4 Tablespoons
cup	5 Tablespoons plus 1 teaspoon
cup	8 Tablespoons
cup	12 Tablespoons
up	16 Tablespoons
ound	16 ounces

US liquid volume measurements

luid ounces	1 Cup
int	2 Cups (= 16 fluid ounces)
uart	2 Pints (= 4 cups)
allon	4 Quarts (= 16 cups)

All cookbooks by Rose M. Ousley are
available on Amazon.com

Made in the USA
Columbia, SC
19 August 2022

65654492R00024